DISCARDED

The Science of

Tools

LIVING SCIENCE

Andrea Munro

Gareth Stevens Publishing
A WORLD ALMANAC EDUCATION GROUP COMPANY

Please visit our web site at: www.garethstevens.com
For a free color catalog describing Gareth Stevens' list of high-quality books and multimedia programs, call 1-800-542-2595 (USA) or 1-800-461-9120 (Canada).
Gareth Stevens Publishing's Fax: (414) 332-3567.

Library of Congress Cataloging-in-Publication Data

Munro, Andrea.
  The science of tools / by Andrea Munro.
    p. cm. – (Living science)
  Includes index.
  ISBN 0-8368-2793-7 (lib. bdg.)
    1. Tools–Juvenile literature. [1. Tools.] I. Title. II. Living science (Milwaukee, Wis.)
  TJ1195 .M82   2001
  621.9–dc21
                                                        00-063754

This edition first published in 2001 by
Gareth Stevens Publishing
A World Almanac Education Group Company
330 West Olive Street, Suite 100
Milwaukee, WI 53212 USA

Project Co-ordinator: Jared Keen
Series Editor: Celeste Peters
Copy Editor: Heather Kissock
Design: Warren Clark
Cover Design: Terry Paulhus
Layout: Lucinda Cage
Gareth Stevens Editor: Jean B. Black

Every reasonable effort has been made to trace ownership and to obtain permission to reprint copyright material. The publishers would be pleased to have any errors or omissions brought to their attention so that they may be corrected in subsequent printings.

Photograph Credits:
Corbis: pages 4, 20 bottom; Corel Corporation: pages 5 left, 6 center, 7 center, 7 right, 8, 15 bottom left, 22, 26, 30 center right, 31 top left; Eyewire: cover (background), page 14 right; Lyn Hancock: page 11 left; Lee Valley Tools: pages 6 center left, 9 center; Dr. Gerald Newlands: page 11 right; Bryan Pezzi: pages 12 center, 13 left, 18 center; PhotoDisc: cover (center), pages 6 left, 6 center right, 6 right, 7 left, 7 center left, 7 center right, 13 bottom right, 14 left, 15 top right, 17 center, 18 left, 20 left, 21 center; Monique de St. Croix: pages 12 right, 13 center, 15 bottom right, 16, 17 top, 19, 21 right, 21 bottom left, 27, 29, 30 left, 30 bottom right, 31 center, 31 bottom left; Visuals Unlimited: pages 5 right (Joe McDonald), 9 top (John Sohlden), 9 bottom (Roger Cole), 23 (Jon Bertsch), 24 (C. P. Hickman), 25 (Hal Beral), 28 (Arthur Morris), 31 top right (L.S. Stepanowicz).

Printed in the United States of America

1 2 3 4 5 6 7 8 9 05 04 03 02 01

Contents

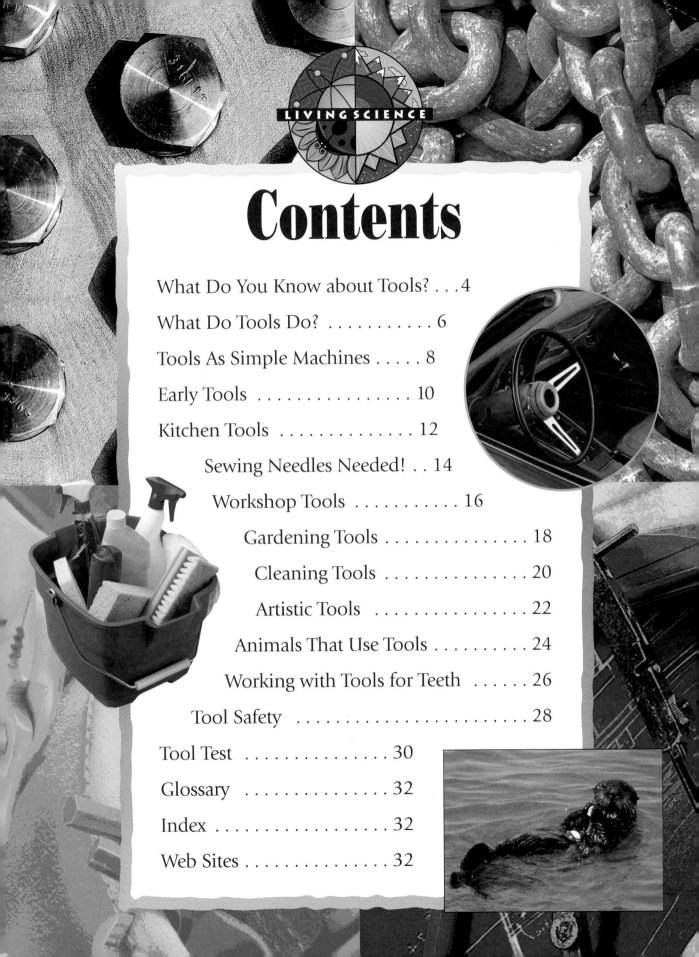

What Do You Know about Tools?

Imagine life without fire, clothing, or shelter. Nights would be very cold and dark. We could not live where it snows in winter. There would be no walls to protect us from wild animals. Our world would be very different if we did not have tools.

Tools help people do things. They help pound, cut, dig, scrape, spread, grip, turn, gather, lift, move, and join items. Hand tools need energy from people to make them work. Power tools run on electricity, fuel, or some other source of energy.

Human energy makes a hammer pound nails.

Why are people able to make and use tools? Human hands are good at holding onto things. We can touch our thumbs to our other fingers, so we can grip things much better than most other animals can. A human also has a large brain. The brain helps a person imagine how to use objects as tools. It also allows the person to design and create those tools.

This drill is a power tool that runs on electrical energy.

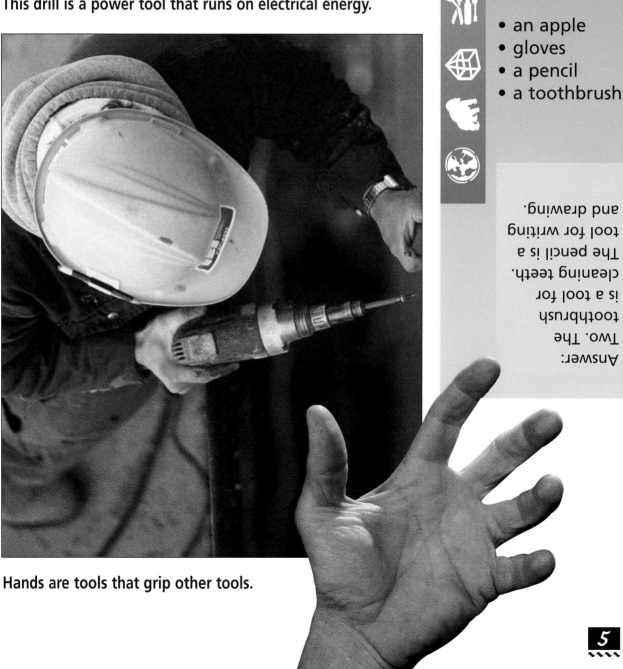

Hands are tools that grip other tools.

Puzzler

How many of the following objects are tools?

- an apple
- gloves
- a pencil
- a toothbrush

Answer: Two. The toothbrush is a tool for cleaning teeth. The pencil is a tool for writing and drawing.

What Do Tools Do?

Tools can be grouped by what they do. Many of the tools listed on the chart below were invented more than 5,000 years ago. How these tools look might have changed over the years, but they are still used to do the same kinds of work.

What Tools Do

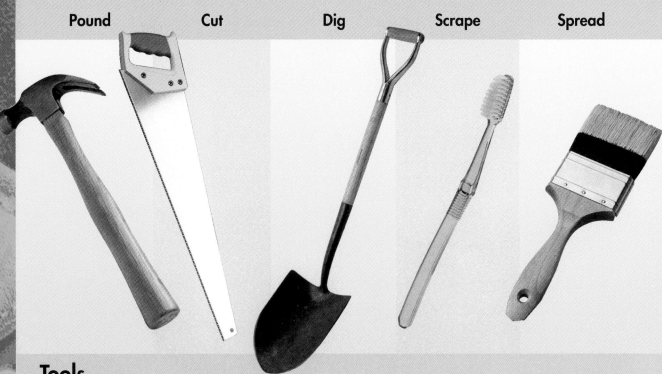

Pound	Cut	Dig	Scrape	Spread

Tools

Pound	Cut	Dig	Scrape	Spread
hammer, mallet, rock, sledgehammer	saw, ax, knife, razor blade, scissors, sickle	shovel, cultivator, garden trowel, hoe, pick	toothbrush, chisel, file, sandpaper	paintbrush, pen, pencil, putty knife, spatula

Activity

Build a Cool Tool Scrapbook

Look through magazines. Find a picture of one tool from each group listed on the chart. Ask your parents if you may cut out the pictures. Then arrange and paste the pictures in a scrapbook.

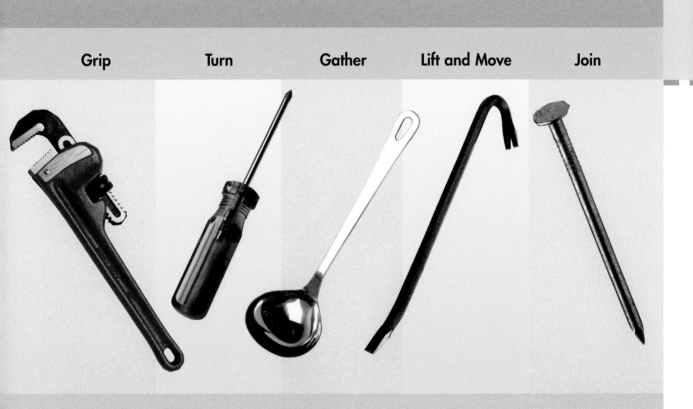

Grip	Turn	Gather	Lift and Move	Join
wrench, pliers, nutcracker, tongs, vise	screwdriver, crank, wheel and axle	ladle, broom, pitchfork, rake, spoon	crowbar, jack, pulley, ramp, winch	nail, needle and thread, nut and bolt, screw, staple

Tools As Simple Machines

A few tools are called simple machines. These tools are the building blocks we use to make complex machines. All machines that have moving parts, from clocks to cars, are made of one or more simple machines.

A Lever
lifts heavy weights.
It is a bar that turns on a kind of support called a **fulcrum**. A crane is a lever.

A Wheel and Axle
work together to make things move.
A wheel and axle are attached to each other. They turn together to lift or move objects. A car has wheels and axles that help it move. It also has a wheel and axle for steering.

A Pulley
is a lifting tool.
It lifts an object up when a rope is pulled down. Elevators, cranes, and ships use pulleys.

An Inclined Plane

is a sloping surface that helps raise or lower heavy loads. A dump truck uses an inclined plane to dump its load.

A Wedge
has two inclined planes that work together. The planes force their way into a material. The sharp edge of an ax is a wedge that can chop through wood.

A Screw
is an inclined plane that winds around a pole like a spiral staircase. When a screw is turned, its spiraled plane easily moves into or out of a material.

Puzzler

Which type of simple machine is each of the following tools?

- an ax
- a corkscrew
- a nutcracker
- a wheelchair ramp

Answer: An ax is a wedge. A corkscrew is a screw. A nutcracker is two levers working together. A wheelchair ramp is an inclined plane.

Early Tools

People began to use tools thousands of years ago. Their first tools were objects they found, such as sticks, bones, and stones. Over time, people thought of ways to make better tools from these objects. For example, they tied stones to wooden handles to make hammers. They sharpened stones and tied them to long sticks to make spears.

When people started farming, they needed a whole new set of tools. They made sharp curved blades, called sickles, for cutting grain. They wove baskets for gathering crops. They made large clay pots for storing food.

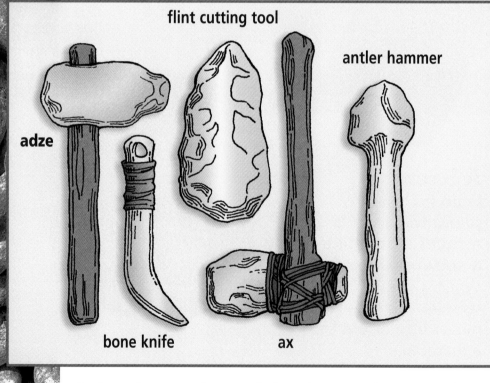

flint cutting tool

antler hammer

adze

bone knife

ax

Early tools were often made by tying two objects together.

Later, people made metal tools. The metals they used were copper, bronze, and iron. Metal tools were stronger and lasted longer than tools made from stone or bone. Many modern tools are similar to these early tools and are still made from iron, in a form known as steel.

A fire can be started using simple tools to create sparks. Ancient ways to start fires still work today.

A sharp wood spearhead was a valuable tool for early hunters.

Puzzler

Which tool was one of our most important early inventions? Clue: It turns.

Answer:
The wheel and axle. With this tool, people could move heavy loads long distances. With a potter's wheel, people could make clay pots for storing food.

Kitchen Tools

People need many tools for cooking and eating. They use pots and pans to hold food that must be cooked. Dishes, such as plates and bowls, hold the food while they eat it.

Some animals have big teeth for tearing their food. People have small teeth, so they use knives to cut their food. Forks and spoons help them gather the food and put it in their mouths.

A vegetable peeler (left) has sharp wedges that can cut the skin off a potato. Tongs (below) are levers that grip food.

A kitchen contains many **specialized** tools. A rolling pin flattens dough. A funnel guides liquid into the small opening of a bottle. A potato masher crushes cooked potatoes and other soft foods. A juicer squeezes the juice out of fruits and vegetables.

Sometimes people use electric tools in the kitchen. They might use an electric **mixer**, for example, to whip cream. They could also use a hand **whisk** to make whipped cream, but it would take a long time, and their wrists would get tired!

Activity

Cookie Tool Tally

Make cookies and count the tools you use to make them. Did you use a cookie cutter? How many tools did you use that needed electricity?

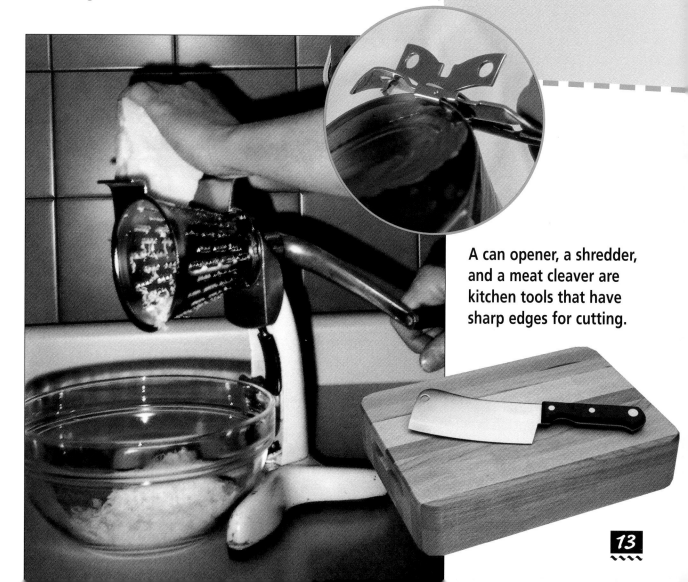

A can opener, a shredder, and a meat cleaver are kitchen tools that have sharp edges for cutting.

Sewing Needles Needed!

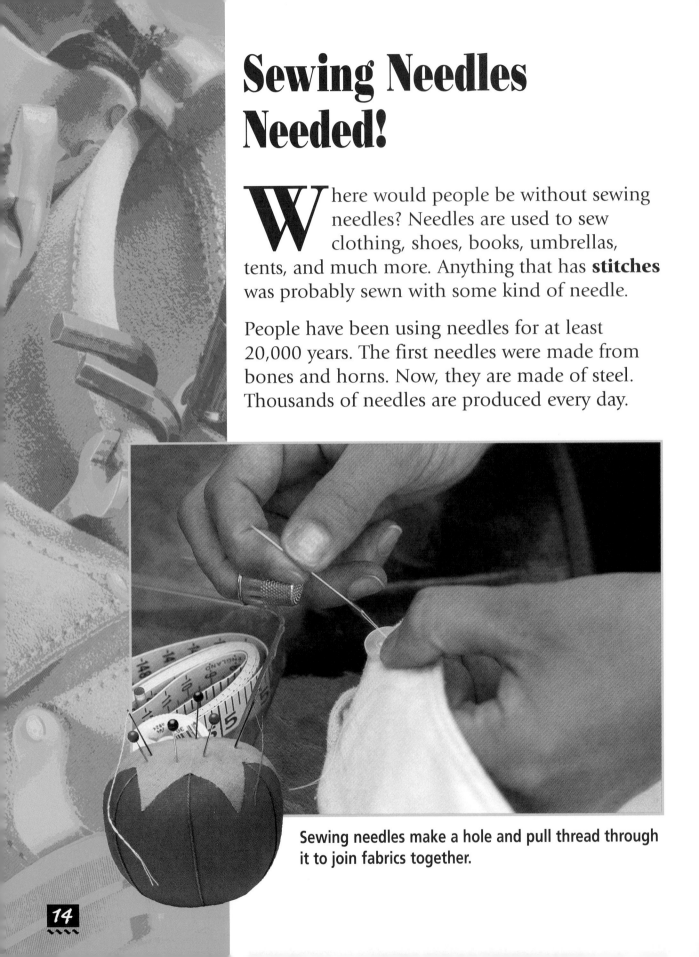

Where would people be without sewing needles? Needles are used to sew clothing, shoes, books, umbrellas, tents, and much more. Anything that has **stitches** was probably sewn with some kind of needle.

People have been using needles for at least 20,000 years. The first needles were made from bones and horns. Now, they are made of steel. Thousands of needles are produced every day.

Sewing needles make a hole and pull thread through it to join fabrics together.

Although steel needles are simple tools, it takes several machines to **manufacture** them. One machine holds each needle and turns it, while another machine sharpens the point. A third machine flattens a place where the hole, or eye, will be punched, and a fourth machine makes the hole.

All sewing used to be done by hand. Then, in 1846, Elias Howe invented the sewing machine. People powered the first sewing machines by rocking a foot pedal back and forth. Modern sewing machines have electric motors for power.

Sewing machines help people sew more quickly and easily than they could by hand.

Puzzler

One type of needle is never used for sewing. Can you guess which type?

Answer: The needle a doctor or a nurse uses to give a person a shot.

Different kinds of needles are made for different uses.

Workshop Tools

A workshop is a place to build and **repair** things. Many tools are kept there to do whatever job comes along. Imagine that you wanted to build a wooden toy in the workshop. Which tools would you need?

First, you would need a saw to cut blocks of wood into different shapes and sizes. A workshop often has many saws. Some saws cut wood, and others cut metal. Some cut circles, while others cut only straight lines. All saws have sharp teeth. Anyone using a saw should keep hands and fingers away from these teeth.

Cutting a board is easier when the board is held firmly in place. A vise can grip an object, such as this board, tightly.

After the wooden shapes are cut, they have to be smoothed. Many tools make things smooth. A **rasp** makes wood smooth, while a file makes steel smooth. The rough surface of sandpaper smooths and polishes wood.

To finish the toy, the wooden shapes need to be nailed together. Most workshops have hammers and nails. They also have many other useful tools. Pliers can be used to bend and cut wires. Screwdrivers tighten screws. Wrenches hold bolts in place and tighten nuts. Power drills make holes in wood and metal.

Carpenters use all kinds of tools, including hammers and pliers.

Puzzler

A hammer and a mallet are both used for pounding. Which one would you use to pound metal nails into wood?

Answer: A hammer is used to pound metal nails into wood. You would use a mallet to pound softer objects, such as wooden pegs, into wood.

Gardening Tools

Do you like to dig in the dirt? If you do, there are many tools that can help you. Shovels and spades have long handles and metal blades with sharp edges. They are used for digging and moving dirt.

A cultivator is a tool with clawlike hooks attached to a handle. It is used to loosen dirt.

Garden trowels are like small shovels with curved edges and short handles. They are used to move plants from one place to another.

Tools help us do many other things in the garden besides dig. Rakes help us gather leaves and grass clippings. Power lawn mowers cut grass quickly and evenly. Pruners are used to cut dead branches off of trees. Shears, which look like big scissors, help us cut **hedges** and flowers.

Activity

Digging Around
Find out how useful gardening tools are. Try digging a hole in your backyard using just your hands. Next, use a stick. Then, try a shovel. Which way was the easiest?

A bulb planter (left) makes a hole just the right size and depth for planting a flower bulb. Then, a garden trowel (above) can be used to fill the hole with dirt.

Cleaning Tools

Houses. Cars. Clothes. Dishes. Everything people use needs to be cleaned sooner or later. Soap and water can clean almost anything, but there are tools that can do a better job. Most of them are also easier to use.

Cleaning the house often begins with dusting. Soft rags or feather dusters can be used to wipe the dust off furniture and window sills. The floors come next. They can be swept with a broom, mopped, or cleaned with an electric vacuum cleaner.

Cleaning tools make getting dirt out easier.

A bristle brush is a handy cleaning tool. It works well for scrubbing dried mud off of a shoe. A bristle brush, however, is not good for cleaning every surface. A rag or a sponge is a better tool for cleaning something that is easily scratched, such as a sink or a faucet. An even softer cloth, called a chamois, is best for polishing furniture and cars.

We use brushes, dishcloths, and scouring pads to clean in the kitchen. Their rough surfaces help loosen food stuck to dishes and pots.

Activity

Tool Hunt

Look around your house. Find at least five tools that are used to clean only one thing. For example, a pet comb is never used on anything but pets!

A fireplace needs its own set of tools.

Artistic Tools

Writers and artists often use pencils, pens, and brushes. These tools help them make lasting records of their thoughts and feelings.

The first tools for writing and painting were brushes. Early brushes were made of plants or feathers or animal hair. Today, artists still use brushes made of animal hair, but many brushes are made of nylon **fibers**. These fibers are very strong, and they bend easily.

A pencil contains a thin rod of **graphite**. Graphite is a dark carbon material that rubs off on paper. The graphite is enclosed in wood, metal, or plastic to keep it from rubbing off on fingers.

Artists use brushes, pencils, and pens to create their masterpieces.

The first pens were made from plants with hollow stems, called reeds. Later, the sharpened spines of feathers were used. These early pens had to be dipped in ink. Today, people use ballpoint pens, which have an ink supply inside them. A little ball at the end of the pen helps the ink roll out smoothly onto paper.

Pens and brushes are used in calligraphy. Calligraphy is artistic writing.

Puzzler

People once used a type of food as an eraser. Can you guess which food? Clue: It is soft and smells delicious.

Answer:
The inside of fresh bread was rolled into a ball and used as an eraser!

Animals That Use Tools

Humans are not the only animals that use tools. Chimpanzees, ants, birds — even fish — use tools to find and catch food.

Chimpanzees use many different tools. They crumple up leaves to make cups for water and to clean themselves. They use branches to rake their food closer to them. Sometimes chimpanzees make the branches sharper by chewing on the ends. A sharp tool can be very useful.

For some birds, a small stick is a tool for picking insects out of tree bark.

Some ants use leaves, wood, and mud as gathering tools. With these tools, they can lift and carry soft food, such as honey.

When a woodpecker-finch holds a twig in its beak and pushes it underneath tree bark, the bird is looking for insects to eat. The Egyptian vulture is another bird that uses tools. It picks up stones with its beak and throws them at ostrich eggs, trying to break an egg.

Archerfish use water as a tool to catch **prey**. They go after spiders and insects resting near or flying over the water. The fish shoots a stream of water out of its mouth to knock its prey into the water.

Sea otters use rocks to crack open shellfish.

Activity

Monkey Business
Next time you are at the zoo, watch the apes and monkeys. Are they using tools? What are they using the tools for? Are they scratching or defending themselves, or bringing food closer to them?

25

Working with Tools for Teeth

When you think about a dentist's office, what sound comes to mind? A drill! Dentists use drills and many other tools to clean and repair teeth. They learn how to use these tools in a school of dentistry. The tools help dentists work in areas of a person's mouth where fingers cannot reach.

Dentists often use more than one tool at a time.

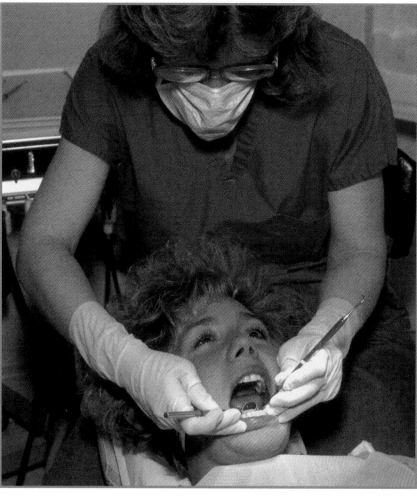

Dentists check for cavities and gum problems using a tool called an explorer. This tool has a very sharp, pointed end. It can poke into tiny places. Dentists also use small mirrors with long handles to help them see the upper teeth and the backs of teeth.

When a dentist finds a cavity, the drilling begins. The dentist drills away the rotting part of the tooth, then plugs the clean hole with a filling. A tool called a carver shapes the filling to fit the tooth. The carver makes a squeaking sound.

Buzzing drills and squeaking carvers — would you like to work with tools for teeth?

A scaler scrapes plaque off of teeth.

Activity

Do Your Own Research

Have a parent or a teacher help you find out more about the following careers in which tools are used:

- carpenter
- chef
- dental hygienist
- landscaper
- machinist
- mechanic
- surgeon
- toolmaker

To help prevent tooth decay, special holders keep **fluoride** around teeth until it is absorbed.

27

Tool Safety

Tools can be dangerous. Many have sharp edges, points, or teeth. Some can pinch, crush, or scrape. Tools must be used carefully. It is important to hold and use tools properly. It is also wise to wear **protective** clothing while using tools. Gloves, safety goggles, and boots help guard against harm.

A sharp knife is safer than a dull one. Because you must push harder on a dull knife to make it cut, it is more difficult to stop the blade before it reaches your hand.

Stay safe around tools. Follow these simple rules.

1. Hang tools on the wall to keep them out of the way. People often get hurt when tools are left laying around.
2. Wash sharp kitchen knives separately from other dishes.
3. Put knives away in a knife holder that covers the blades. Make sure each knife has its own covering before placing it in a drawer. This way, you will not cut yourself the next time you reach into the drawer for something.
4. Carry scissors and other sharp objects with the sharp ends pointed away from you.
5. Always ask someone to teach you how to use a tool properly before you try to use it.

This man knows to keep his legs out of the way of the ax.

Tool Test

Tools can be used for many purposes, from gripping to gathering. Try to match each of the following labels with the picture of the tool that does that kind of work.

Grip

Cut

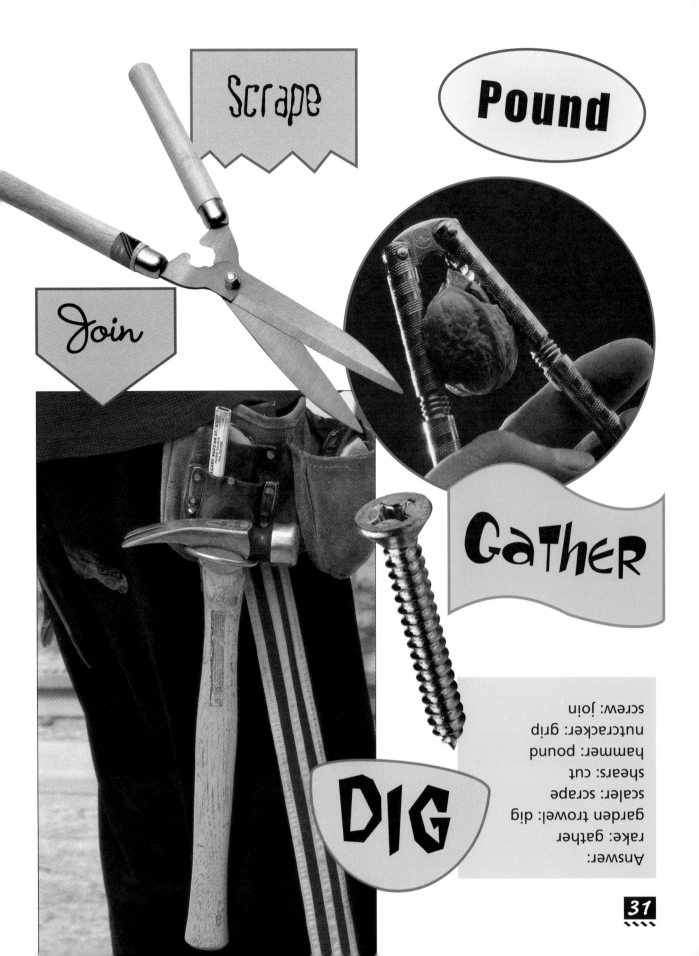

Scrape

Pound

Join

Gather

DIG

Glossary

adze: a type of ax used mainly to shape wood.

fibers: threads.

fluoride: a chemical that helps prevent cavities from forming in teeth.

fulcrum: the support on which a lever rests.

graphite: a soft mineral that leaves a black mark on objects it touches.

hedges: rows of bushes planted close together.

manufacture: make something, especially in a factory.

mixer: a kitchen tool that mixes foods together.

plaque: a sticky film that forms on and around teeth and contains bacteria that cause tooth decay.

prey: an animal that is hunted and killed for food.

protective: helping to keep safe from harm.

rasp: a file with rough teeth for smoothing wood.

repair: fix.

specialized: made to do one particular thing.

stitches: threads sewn in and out of pieces of material to join them together.

whisk: a kitchen tool used for whipping liquids.

Index

Web Sites

sln.fi.edu/qa97/spotlight3/spotlight3.html

tqjunior.thinkquest.org/6400/tools.htm

www.antiquetools.com/10-tools/index.html

www.exploratorium.edu/cycling/wheel1.html

Some web sites stay current longer than others. For further web sites, use your search engines to locate the following topics: *gardening tools, kitchen supplies, wheels,* and *workshops.*